Stock Market Investing

The Complete Beginner's Guide to Gain Passive Income by Stock Market Investing (Learn Secret Hints and Tips to Make Your Money Work for You!)

John James

© Copyright 2018 by John James

All rights reserved.

The following eBook is reproduced below with the goal of providing information that is as accurate and reliable as possible. Regardless, purchasing this eBook can be seen as consent to the fact that both the publisher and the author of this book are in no way experts on the topics discussed within and that any recommendations or suggestions that are made herein are for entertainment purposes only. Professionals should be consulted as needed prior to undertaking any of the action endorsed herein.

This declaration is deemed fair and valid by both the American Bar Association and the Committee of Publishers Association and is legally binding throughout the United States.

Furthermore, the transmission, duplication or reproduction of any of the following work including specific information will be considered an illegal act irrespective of if it is done electronically or in print. This extends to creating a secondary or tertiary copy of the work or a recorded copy and is only allowed with express written consent from the Publisher. All additional rights reserved.

The information in the following pages is broadly considered to be a truthful and accurate account of facts and as such any inattention, use or misuse of the information in question by the reader will render any resulting actions solely under their purview. There are no scenarios in which the publisher or the original author of this work can be in any fashion deemed liable for any hardship or damages that may befall them after undertaking information described herein.

Additionally, the information in the following pages is intended only for informational purposes and should thus be thought of as universal. As befitting its nature, it is presented without assurance regarding its prolonged validity or interim quality. Trademarks that are mentioned are done without written consent and can in no way be considered an endorsement from the trademark holder.

Table of Contents

Chapter 1: The Right Mindset Makes All the Difference 7

Chapter 2: Picking Out Stocks to Invest In 15

Chapter 3: How to Purchase Stocks 27

Chapter 4: What Options Do I Have For Stock Market Investing? 32

Chapter 5: Picking Out Your Investment Strategy 43

Chapter 6: Different Styles That Expert Traders Use for Stock Trading 60

Chapter 7: Rules That Help to Reduce Your Risks When Investing in the Stock Market 70

Conclusion 83

Introduction

Congratulations on downloading this book and thank you for doing so.

The following chapters will discuss everything you need to know to get started with investing in the stock market. While some people will choose to start their own businesses, work on their retirements, or work in real estate investing, there is nothing that works as well, and provides the return on investment, as when you work in the stock market.

This guidebook will talk about everything that you need to know to get started with investing in the stock market. We will talk about the mindset that you need to see success with the stock market investment, how to pick out stocks that will provide a good return on investment, how to enter the stock market, how to pick good strategies, and how to reduce your risk. Whether you have been an investor in the past or not, this guidebook will help you to get started in the stock market.

There are plenty of books on this subject on the market, thanks again for choosing this one! Every effort was made to ensure it is full of as much useful information as possible, please enjoy!

Chapter 1: The Right Mindset Makes All the Difference

When it comes to investing your money and putting it to work for you, there are several opportunities that you can choose from. Each person has their own personal style when it comes to these investments and picking out the one that is best for their needs. Some people might like to get their hands dirty and follow the market with real estate investing. Some like to play it safe and will just put their money into a retirement plan. And others will choose to work with the stock market.

Often it will depend on how much time you have to devote to the investment, how much money you can put towards the investment, and how much risk you are willing to take. Of course, the more risk you are willing to take, the more money you could potentially make. There is also the risk of losing more money, which is why you need to find the perfect balance between how much you can earn with an investment and how much you could lose with that investment if things go wrong.

While there are a lot of different investment opportunities that you can choose from, such as real estate investing, investing in bonds, starting your own business and more, you can also work with the stock market. This type of investment will include you taking your money and investing it to help another company grow. In return for investing in a company that does well, you will earn dividends each quarter, or part of the profit that the company brings in. Or you could get into the process of buying the stocks at a lower price and selling them when the price goes up so that you can make a profit.

Those are the two most common ways to make money in the stock market, but there are many others that you can work with as well. With all the options available for investing in the stock market, it is no wonder that a lot of people choose to go with this option. You will be able to take a look at how much time, money, and risk you have available and choose which stocks, as well as which strategies, will be the best for you. Depending on which stocks you go with, it is even possible to start making a profit without all the wait.

It is exciting to get into the stock market and see how things can go for you, but some people want to weigh all their options and make sure that they can actually make money rather than losing out on money. When you are ready to start entering the stock market, and you want to make a good income from your investment, make sure to learn the right strategies that will ensure that you see success.

Starting off in the stock market

Before you decide to jump right into stock market investing, you must take some time to determine what your goals are for doing this kind of investing. If you jump into this investment without thinking it through, you will fail miserably. You should know where you want to start out at as well as why you are doing the investment. Do you want to start investing to help your retirement fund, to make a side income, or even to replace your full income? The answer to this will help determine how you will behave when you get into the market.

There are many options that you can choose for goals when you want to invest. Choosing the right one can sometimes help you to figure out how much risk you want to take and which stocks you want to invest in. For example, if you are looking to turn the stock market investment into your full-time income, you may be willing to take on more risk to bring in more money. If you want to make just enough to put some in the bank or pay off a few bills, then it may be best to go with less risky options.

No matter which goal you choose for investing, you will quickly find that the stock market is one of the best options that you can choose for your investment. There are many companies that you can choose to work with, many strategies that work well, and even different levels of risk that you can pick from. You can pick a plan that has a bit more risk that will also help you earn more rewards, or you can take your time to learn more about the stock market and pick less risky options while still making money.

You do need to have a good idea of how the stock market works and how to get into the game before you start. First, we need to understand what a stock is. A stock is a type of security that will give the investor, or you if you choose this option, part ownership in the business that the stock belongs to. This also means that the investor will be able to claim some of the assets and earnings of the business as well. The buyer will be known as a shareholder, and along with some of the other investors, they will be the new owners of that business. The amount of ownership that you have will depend on a number of stocks that you possess. There are also two types of stocks including common stocks and preferred stocks.

How do I trade in stocks?

One of the first questions that you may have as a new investor is how to trade stocks. When you join in on the stock market, you must trade stocks using the stock exchange. This is simply the place where the sellers and buyers of stocks will come together and then agree on the price for a particular stock. There are a few places where you can physically go to do this, but for the most part, you will do your trades online.

Once you get into the stock market and look at it for a bit, you will notice that the prices of each stock will change all the time. Many different factors come into play when determining what the price of the stock will be. These factors change on a regular basis, which is what makes it so hard to keep the prices steady for the long term. For example, if the supply of the stock is pretty high while the demand is low, the price of that stock will stay lower. If the demand for the particular stock goes up and the supply goes down or stays the same, then the price of those stocks will go up as well. The prices of the various stocks will usually be what people in the stock market see as the worth of the stocks and can show how interested people are in purchasing that stock at one time or another.

Not only can you pay attention to the demand and supply of a particular stock, but you will also find that the earnings of the company behind the stock can determine how much it is worth as well. This means that you need to look at how much money the company is able to earn each year. Of course, the exact amount will change from one year to another, so it is a good place to start to see if the company is growing and if you will be able to make some money from the investment. It is easy to find these numbers by looking through some of the financial journals and reports that the company is required to put out in order to be on the stock market.

Keeping track of all the prices on the stock market can be hard, and the fact that there are a lot of reasons that these stock prices will change can be a hassle as well. You have to look at some of the changes that the company has recently made or will make soon. Addtionally, you need to look at how well the economy is doing at the time. What this all means is that you do need to do some research. Those who just jump right into the stock market and don't pay attention to what is going on around them are more likely to fail and lose a lot of money.

There is no rush when getting into the stock market. You can do this on your own time and do some thorough research to make sure you are picking out the right stocks and not just risking everything. Finding a good stockbroker to help you along the way can make the process so much easier as well.

Chapter 2: Picking Out Stocks to Invest In

After taking some time to research the stock market and what it has to offer, it is important that you take the time to pick out the right stocks. There are thousands of companies available on the stock market, but not all of them will provide you with a good return on investment. Some will provide you with one of the best opportunities to make money without all the risk and others will be failures right from the beginning. As a beginner, you may be worried about how you will sort these out so that you can pick the right stocks to make the most money for you.

The first thing that you should look at when you are ready to join the stock market is that you should never just pick out a stock, no matter what the circumstances are, simply because you heard through the grapevine or from a friend of a friend that the stock was a good one. Doing your own research is important. You can take the advice of other people, such as friends who are in the stock market and your broker, but remember that this is your investment and you need to be the one in control of it. Do some of your own research on the market, and you will soon learn which stocks are the best ones for your needs, regardless of what other people say.

If you have already done some research and have come up with a list of companies that you want to look at some more and possibly invest in, make sure to take some time searching on their website. Most of them will have information about their stocks, and this can be helpful when making your decision. You need to take a look at all of their reports on finances if possible to because this tells you how the company has done so far on the market. You will be surprised at how much information you are able to get about a company just by snooping around a little bit.

While there are a lot of things that you will need

to consider when it comes to picking out a stock to work with, you need to go with one that will actually make you money in the process. Never pick a stock that is obviously going to cost you more than you can earn and try to go with the ones that are winners. There are a few things that you can take a look at to limit your risks including:

- The margin of profit for that company.
- The debts that a company has and how much those debts are.
- The return on equity with that company.
- The debt to equity ratio. This is a good thing to look up because it will give you an idea of how this particular company spends their money and whether they do so responsibly or not.
- How the company has done in the past and whether they are expected to do the same, better, or worse.

What should I be looking for?

So, you may be curious about what things you need to look for to pick out a good company to invest in. You will want to spend some time looking through charts and graphs to see how a particular stock has been doing inside the stock market, but that is only one part of the story. You also need to take a look at the company itself to see if it will maintain that status for the long term. For example, there may be a company who looks good when you go through the charts and graphs, but if they are not good at spending money or keeping their debts down, then they are not the company for you. Some of the different things that you should consider looking at when you are ready to pick out a stock includes:

Who manages the business

This is one of the first things that you should look at when you want to start investing in a company. Who manages the business will help you to figure out how the company is doing now as well as how it will do in the future. Many beginners consider the management of a company not all that important. However, if the current management is not doing well with running the company, even a solid company can go downhill fast.

Now, you need to carefully consider the management of a company before you decide to invest in it. There are a few points that you can consider such as what the return on equity is if the shareholders are still earning a profit each year. If the equity return of the company is five percent or higher, it is usually a safe bet that the company will keep growing and doing well. Also, look and see how the management is doing with others and with each other. Are they getting along and making decisions that are good for the company, or is there are a lot of internal fighting that could ruin the company?

Pick a sector that is doing well

When you are picking out stocks, it is important that you find some that come from a business sector that is also doing well. Depending on how the economy is doing, it is possible that some industries will still do well in a downturn, or at least some industries will do better than the rest. There are also times when the economy is doing well, but one or two industries are not doing as well as the rest of the market.

This is why it is so important to pick out industries that are doing well. You may also want to consider spreading your money out a bit so that you can avoid trouble if one of your industries starts to do poorly. And, while it is best to go with industries that are predicted to do well over a long period of time, if you find that one of your industries is not performing the way that you want, it is easy to sell that stock and try something else.

Growing profits

You also need to look for a company that is making profits. If you see a company that is losing money from the start, then it will be hard for you to get a good return on investment. You also want to make sure that the company is getting bigger profits each year. When the company keeps on growing their profits, it is doing well and has a lot of popularity that is growing as well. This makes it a good investment option for many people. The bigger the profits, the better return on investment you will be able to get.

The size of your company

Some investors want to work with a company that is a little bit smaller. They think that these are easier to work with and that they will be able to monitor that company a little bit better than some of the bigger companies. However, there have been some studies done that show how smaller companies will actually carry more risks with them compared to investing in some of the bigger companies.

The reason for this is that a lot of the bigger companies have taken their time to become established. They didn't become big overnight, so you know that they will be safe investments. As a beginner who has never worked in the stock market, it is usually better to go with a company that is bigger and more established. After you have learned how to work in the stock market and you understand the types of risks that you want to take, you can choose to go with a smaller company if you would like.

Also, as a beginner, you should make sure that you are avoiding penny stocks. These sometimes are tempting because they are usually really inexpensive to work with. However, these companies are really risky and often they do not need to provide users and investors with financial information even though they are on the exchange. It is likely that you will lose a lot of money if you choose to work with these penny stocks. It is a better idea to stick with one of the main companies that are on the stock market so that you know they are safer options and you are more likely to make money.

Look at the dividend payments

When you look at a company, check and see if they are able to pay out dividends to their investors. Companies that are able to share their profits already are great options for a beginner to work with. This shows that the company is already able to manage their debts while still sharing the profits with the shareholders. It is likely that they will be able to do it again and you will continue to receive these payments in the future.

Also, when you are deciding how much you can make with dividend payments, you should go with a company that is able to pay you at least two percent. This is a good sign that the company is pretty steady and that you will be able to make a decent amount of money each year. If you can find one that is higher than the two percent, then you are able to make even more in profits.

Manageable debt

While you are taking a look at some of these companies to invest in, you should take a look at the debts that they have. The company doesn't necessarily need to be completely debt free, but they need to have a good balance between the amount of debt that they take on and the amount of profit that they are able to bring out.

There are some good debts that a company will have, especially if they are just starting out or if they have recently undergone an expansion. They may have some debts for their buildings, for their equipment and so much more. You are not likely to find a company that doesn't have any debt, but you should look for one that has kept their debt manageable for the profits that they make each year. If you are looking for a company and they have so much debt that they are barely able to cover it each month, then it is best to go with someone else. In this case, it is unlikely that they will be able to keep managing that debt and you will lose money.

Go with liquid stocks

And finally, another thing that you can consider when you are looking at stocks to invest in is how liquid those stocks are. Liquid stocks are good because these are the ones that you will easily be able to find sellers and buyers for. If you go with a stock that is not liquid, you may find that it is really hard to sell that stock later on when you want to leave the market. Most stocks will have some kind of liquidity with them, but the more liquid the stock is considered, the easier it is for you to sell it when you would like.

Try to find a stock that has a happy medium. You want it to be at a good price, so you do not want the demand for that stock to be too high. If the demand is too high, it will be too expensive to get ahold of it to start. But the demand needs to be high enough that when you are ready to leave the market, no matter what that reason is, you will be able to find someone who is willing to purchase the stocks from you.

There are a lot of things that you will need to consider when it comes to picking out the right stocks for your needs. You should do your research to figure out who is managing the company, how they are doing with their profits and their debts, and find stocks that will be easy to sell if you decide to leave the market. When you are able to do this, you are sure to find some good and secure stocks that will help you to make a good profit.

Chapter 3: How to Purchase Stocks

Earlier, we took some time to explore the things that you should look at to find the perfect stocks to invest in. You want to make sure that you pick out stocks that will actually bring you money, ones that have good management, steady profits, and manageable debts so that you can make money. After you have done some research on the stock market, it is time to enter the market and actually purchase the stocks that you want to invest in. Let's take a look at how you enter the market by purchasing stocks.

Use a broker

Since you are a beginner and you have not had the opportunity to work in the stock market yet, it may be a good idea to work with a broker. The broker will help you make smart decisions when it comes to the stocks that you should invest in. Brokers spend their time learning how to work with the market, and they have been doing work in this industry for many years. They have a lot of experience and expertise that is needed to help you make good decisions. Beginners can really benefit from taking the advice from a broker they trust.

There are actually a few types of brokers that you can choose to work with and it will depend on how much you would like to spend on the broker and how much advice you will end up needing. The first broker that you can work with is a full-service broker. This type of broker will be responsible for managing all of the stocks and purchases that happen on your account. You will be able to consult with them about any purchases that you are considering and the best steps that you can take to grow your portfolio. You can give some instructions and provide your opinion, but they will take over most of the work for your investment for you. If you have no idea what you are doing and you would like someone to hold your hand, the full-service broker is a good option for you.

nother option for brokers is to work with what is known as a discount broker. These brokers will cost you less than a full-service broker, but remember that it also means you will receive fewer services from them. You must put in more time and effort to get your investments done. However, they will help you to save some money and can really assist you to get some of the advice that you need in the investment world.

Consider a reinvestment plan

You can, while you are working on which stocks to go with, decide to work with one individual company. When you work with this company, you can take the profits that you earn through dividends, and then use that money to purchase more stocks through the same company. As you are first getting started, you will find that you may not be able to invest much, which will limit how many stocks you are able to purchase. When you take that money and reinvest it to get more stocks, rather than taking and personally using the money for your own reasons, can help you to get more profit in the future because you will own more stocks. Over time, your money will start to grow more, and it can help to reduce your risk of investing all at the same time.

Direct investing plans

Since you are a new investor, you will be able to choose whether you would like to work with a direct investment plan. With this kind of investment, you would not have to use a broker to make your purchases, which will save you some fees that you would spend on that person. For this one, you will choose to work directly with the individual company that you want to invest in. You will not go through the stock exchange, but rather, you will go through the company directly to purchase your stocks. There will be a few extra fees that will come with using this option, but they are smaller than what you will find with a broker, so it is a good way to save some money.

This one can be considered similar to the last option, but you will still be able to keep the dividends when you are done, rather than reinvesting those profits. You could choose to use that money to purchase more stocks, but it is not necessary to be considered a direct investment plan. You may want to work with this option if you feel like working with only one company and you don't think that working with a broker is necessary.

All of these options will help you to get your foot in the door of the stock market so that you can start to invest and earn a profit. Remember that in the beginning, you will probably only make a little bit of money, and you may even need to bring in a broker to do the work for you if you are confused, but the point is that you get started and find the option that works the best for you. Take a look through some of the options above and find the one that is sure to fit your style and give you the profits that you want.

Chapter 4: What Options Do I Have For Stock Market Investing?

There are quite a few options that you will be able to choose when you are ready to invest in the stock market. You will need to learn how to narrow down the niche and the industry that you want to work in to make things a little bit easier. While it is important to diversify your portfolio at some point, it is best for a new investor to keep things small.

The strategy that you choose to help you start investing will depend on a number of factors. Sometimes it depends on the money that you have to start with and how much you want to make. Sometimes it depends on the amount of risk involved or the research that you have done on the topic. But even when you have a good plan with lots of research, there are reasons why you should be skeptical and take your time with everything. In this chapter, we will talk about some of the options and even some of the niches that you can choose to help you invest in the right stocks for you.

Dividend Stocks

The first strategy that you can choose is to work with dividend stocks, and it works the best if you would like to pick out a long-term investment. Dividend stocks may not make you rich overnight, but it will help you to earn a lot of money consistently over many years. When going with dividend stocks, you want to make sure that you are picking stocks from companies that are doing well now and are projected to do well in the future. There are quite a few companies who will work out well for this, and if you pick the right one, you will be able to enjoy a percentage of the profits from that company each quarter for as long as you hold the stocks.

Now, it is important to realize that not all stocks that are available on the exchange will work with dividends. This means that you need to check with each company before deciding to use them for this process. Screening companies is a good idea as well because this will help you to figure out which companies will actually give you a dividend each quarter (if the company doesn't make a profit, they are not able to provide their shareholders with any dividends). Each company that trades on the stock exchange will need to put out financial statements. Make sure to utilize these to help you make good decisions.

As you go through your research, you should be able to come up with a list of companies that pay their shareholders a decent dividend. But you do not want to start out with too many companies, so it is now time to narrow the list down a little bit to find those that meet all your criteria. Some of the things that you should look into with each company that you are interested in will include:

- Look to see if the company has had a steady history of paying out their dividends. It is not a good thing if there is a lot of missed dividend payments because this could show that there are some major issues with the company. It is best to go through their history as far as possible to see how consistent the dividend payments are.
- The next thing to look for is how high the return on equity is for this company. To make sure that you are picking out a good company, you need to look over the past five years and see a return on equity of at least fifteen percent if not higher.
- Each share that you are considering needs to have rising earnings and sales over time. If the shares are going down, then you know that you will lose money if you go with this stock.
- The dividends that are provided to the shareholders need to grow as well. This means that you will earn more money over

time, instead of getting the exact same amount every year. A good company will see a growth in their dividends of at least five percent over ten years.

Take a look at the list of companies that you are interested in and check to see if they meet some of the requirements above. If they do, then they are a great option to go with, and you should consider investing your money in them.

Foreign stock investing

Another option that you can choose to go with is the foreign stock investing. This is an option that most beginners do not stick with because it is hard to follow what is going on in a foreign market. This means that if you want to go into this type of market, you need to do some extra research and pay special attention to what is going on in other countries. If you do this process correctly, there are a lot of companies overseas that are promising and can bring in more money than you can get in your own country. However, it is important to realize that some risks come with working with foreign stock investing.

There are actually a few benefits that you can enjoy when it comes to investing in foreign stocks. Some of the benefits that you will enjoy with these stock options include:

- The stocks that are available in foreign markets will provide you with some new investment opportunities. Based on your goals for investing, it sometimes is a little hard to find a company that you want to invest in, especially if you limit yourself to your own country. You may find that it is easier to find the right investments when you look in other markets.
- Foreign stocks can be a good option for those who are looking for new ways to diversify their portfolios. This can help you to spread out some of your risks, so consider investing your money into a variety of companies, even if you are looking at foreign markets.

While these benefits are really tempting for a beginner who wants to find lucrative companies to invest in, it is important to remember that working in a foreign market actually provides a much higher risk than working in the stock exchange in your market. Even if the company looks like a good and safe investment, it is important to take into account the exchange rate. Depending on which market you go into and the amount of dividend that you expect to make, the cost of exchanging the currency over to USD may take all your profits, which makes the risk of investing in these markets higher than before.

The market conditions are often going to be very different in another country compared to what is going on in your country. For example, the United States may be seeing an upturn in their economy while other countries deal with economies that are shaky. It does not matter what is going on in your home country; what matters is what is going on in whatever country you would like to invest in. This can be good news if the economy in your home country is doing poorly, but it is still something to be aware of.

While there is a lot of potential to make a high profit when you decide to invest in a foreign market, it is very risky, and that is why a lot of beginners choose to not go with this option at all. It may be a good idea to find a good broker and get some help if you decide to go with this as your investment option.

Penny stocks

Penny stocks are an option for investing that some people like to work with, but you have to realize that these are really risky. Beginners like these stocks because they are less expensive than some of the bigger names that are on the stock exchange. If you do not have a lot of money to get started with for this investment, the penny stocks can be a good option for you to go with because you may be better able to afford them.

It is important to realize that not all the companies on the penny stock exchange are reputable. These companies do not need to disclose financial information, and they do not need to meet the same requirements thatcompanies on the stock exchange need to. While there are some companies who will sell shares on this exchange to help them out while they are trying to meet the requirements of the stock exchange (and these are often really good companies to consider because their prices will go up), there are also a lot of failing companies that are working as penny stocks.

This can make it hard to know who you should work with. These penny stocks are really risky, and it is not always the best idea for a beginner to get into this market. Sometimes the value of the stock is hard to figure out, and even a little bit of negative movement can cause a big impact on your investment. Many times these companies are able to hide information from you, and you can lose out your whole investment in no time.

These stocks are really volatile as well, which makes it harder to watch the market and make good decisions.

If you are a beginner and you are interested in checking out penny stocks and learning how they work, then you need to be careful and fully aware of all the risks that come with it. Some of the guidelines that you can consider following when you want to get into penny stocks and still see a return on your investment include:

- Pay attention to some of the warnings that you see. There are some regulators on this market, and if they are sending out some warnings about a particular company, it is worth your time to pay attention.
- Don't always believe what you see. These companies are not held up to the same standards as companies on the stock exchange are. Do your own research and learn as much about the company as possible.

- Learn some more about how penny stocks work. We talked briefly about them, but it is so important to take a look at these stocks and learn more about them before you enter the market.
- Some companies will offer penny stocks, but they are not going to provide you with a lot of information. The less information that is present in a company, the bigger the risk there is to invest in them. Double check that a company is as honest as possible with their information, especially financial information, before you decide to invest.

These are some of the main options that you can work with when you are ready to invest your money in the stock market. Make sure to look through each category and decide which one is the best for your needs.

Chapter 5: Picking Out Your Investment Strategy

Now that we have spent some time looking at all the different options that you have available when picking out a stock, it is time to pick out the strategy that you want to use when it is time to invest in the stock market. There are various strategies that you can work with, and all of them can help you to earn money. The biggest issue with the investment strategy is that you need to fully understand how it works. If you don't understand the strategy or you keep mixing it up with other ones, you will not see success.

So, the first thing that we need to do here is to learn a bit more about the different investment strategies that you can choose from. There are a lot of options, but you must understand how they work if you want any hope for success. Let's take a look at some of the most popular investment strategies and how they should work.

Working with the fundamental analysis

The first investment strategy that we will look at is called a fundamental analysis. This is an easy option to work with, but it does take some time, and you will need to bring out some of your research skills. The goal of working with this kind of analysis is that you want to look at the company that you want to invest in and then figure out what the intrinsic value of that company is. This means that you want to figure out how much the stock of that company is worth when compared to the current value that the company has on the stock exchange.

If the intrinsic value of that company is already higher than what the company is currently trading for, it is a good idea to make a purchase of that stock. When this happens, it means that there is a high likelihood that the stock will go up in price in the near future and you will make money if you enter into the trade at the right time.

Next on the list to figure out is which method you would like to use to help you figure out the intrinsic value of our chosen company. There may be some similarities between these methods, but it is important to pick one. First, you could start out by taking a look at the sum of the discounted cash flows for that company. What this means is that the company will be worth all its future profits when you add them together. Then you can take these projected future profits and discount them so that you can account for what is known as time value, or the force that says that $1 today will be worthless when you get to the future because of inflation.

The idea of the intrinsic value of the company being equal to the future profit will help you to understand how a company can provide more value to its owners. Think about owning your own business and how its worth will include all the money that you can take in as profit when you get to the end of the year. This is only going to be possible if you make a profit after you pay your debts, salaries, suppliers, and other bills first and then have some money left over. This is what you want to find when you look at a company to invest in.

So, where are you going to find some of these numbers? You should be able to find these directly from the company and their financial reports. These reports are required before the company is able to join the stock exchange, which makes it easy for you to take a look through them. You should also take some time to dig deeper and look at the news about a particular company to figure out what numbers are being announced to the public. When you are able to bring all of this information together, it is much easier to help you go through this analysis and pick out the companies that are best for you.

Value investing

Another option or strategy that you can go with when you are ready to invest in the stock market is called value investing. This is actually a really popular strategy that you can try out because it is so successful. When you work with value investing, you will go with a company that has really strong fundamentals, such as strong book value, cash flow, dividends, and earnings. You will then take all that information and compare it to what the stocks are selling for on the market.

When you are a value investor, you will need to look for companies which are undervalued on the market, no matter what the reason, compared to their fundamentals. When a company is undervalued, it means that you are able to purchase their stocks for a great price. As long as the fundamentals of that company are strong, it is very likely that the price of those stocks will increase to their market value, and sometimes higher, once everyone else catches on. You can make a lot of good money with this option as long as you pick a company that fits the bill and you get on it quickly.

Now, it is important to realize that there is a difference between a junk stock and one that is undervalued. If you go with the junk stocks just because they are lower in price, you will end up in some trouble. When you are looking through the market, there are always some companies who will have lower-priced stocks. This is not because those companies are undervalued, but because these companies are just not worth all that much. These companies could have some other issues with them, such as high debt to profit ratio, bad management, or some other reason that they are not worth much.

When you are looking at value stocks, you are looking at companies that actually have good dividends, low debt, and a strong earning potential. Often there is something in the market that is working against them, and so the value of the stock is discounted temporarily. If this is true about the company, then it is likely that their value will go up in no time.

Some beginners do not like to work with value investing. They may feel that most stocks will be at the price where they should be and that it does not matter what the fundamentals are. They may figure that if a stock is supposed to be ranked at a higher price, then it would be at that higher price. There are some investors, on the other hand, who like this method because it helps them to find some good stock investments without having to jump in too late in the game.

CAN SLIM

You can also try using a strategy that goes under the acronym of CAN SLIM. This one will take on a few extra steps to help you see success, but it may be just what a beginner needs to ensure that they are doing the proper research before picking out a new stock to invest in. Let's take a look at what all of these parts mean and how they can help you to pick out a good stock to invest in.

C = Current earnings

With this part, you need to look at the company and see how much they are earning now in the present. You can look at the most recent quarter of the company and then see how it compares to what was made in that same quarter the year before. If this is a solid company, then you should notice that the profits went up from one year to the next. If the profits went down, the company could be experiencing some issues that you want to avoid. It is a good idea to see a growth of twenty percent or more to ensure that you have less risk in the investment.

A = Annual earnings

Now, we will take a look at how much earnings for the company have grown over the past year. You should not just look over one year, though. It is best to look through at least the past five years, if not more, of that company. When you are looking through these five years, you should see that each year has at least a little bit of growth. It is ideal if the growth over the full five years is about twenty-five percent if not more.

N = New

You can also take a look at the company and then find out if some new changes occurred within the company. There are a lot of changes that a business can go through - some will harm the company, and others are good for the company. If you see that some of the harmful changes are being implemented, it is best to leave that organization behind. But if there are some changes in a product being released or within management, it could increase the value of the corporation in the near future.

S = supply and demand

For this criteria, you must take a look at how the supply and the demand of that company is doing. This helps you to know how much the price of the stock is likely to go up in the future. If all things are considered equal in the market, it is easier for some of the smaller firms, who will have fewer shares, to show more gains compared to the bigger ones. The reason for this is because the larger companies will need to deal with a higher demand than some smaller companies just to get it to show up as gains at all.

L = Leader

Here we will take a look at the leaders and the laggards in the market and see how these are able to change your decisions. No matter which industry you will work in, there will be some companies who are considered the leaders. These are the ones that will provide the best dividends to their shareholders. Conversely, there are a few companies who will be lagging behind in the industry, and they are not able to provide a good return on investment to their shareholders. Make sure that you are picking out a company that will be one of the leaders if you would like to make the most money possible.

I = Institutional Sponsorship

The reason that you want to work with institutional sponsorship is because you will be able to see that the company is popular. If you are looking for a company and it doesn't have this kind of sponsorship at all, this means that many money managers have decided not to use this company and there is usually a big red flag reason why they didn't. It is best to pick out a company that has a minimum of three of these institutional owners.

You do need to be watchful if a company has too many of these institutions involved in the process. There is such a thing as a company being owned too much by institutions, and when this happens, it means it is too late for you to get into this company. If you do get into the company, you will probably lose out when those institutions decide to sell the company off. You want a few money managers to be involved, but not too many that it all becomes too congested.

M = Market direction

And the final thing that you will take a look at is the market direction. Any time that you wish to look at a new stock, it is important to look through the market conditions and figure out whether you are dealing with a bear or a bull market. If you do not understand where the market is heading, this will cause a big amount of risk to your gains, and it will be much easier to make some bad decisions on your investment.

Income investing

Another option that you can choose when you are picking out an investment strategy is known as income investing. With income investing, you need to look over the company and then decide whether they are able to provide you with a fairly steady stream of income. This is an easier method, and many beginners like to work with it. When you think about the investment as a way to make a steady income, instead of a way to make money quickly, it is easier to pick out less risky options. There are a variety of options that you would be able to work with for this, such as bonds and fixed income security. There are a number of stocks that can also do this as long as you pick the right one.

To make the income investment work for you, you must be careful that you pick out stocks that will provide a dividend that will be around for a long time. Remember that the average yield for most dividend stocks will be somewhere around three percent. But if you are looking to use this dividend as a way to make an income, then you need to go with a stock that can provide you with a profit of six percent, if not higher, or you are wasting your time.

Of course, in addition to looking through the market and picking out the stocks that will provide you with a steady income stream, you also need to read through the policies that the company releases about the dividends. This can be important because some companies will not keep handing out the dividends in the future. You can also look through this information to see whether the company added some more dividends as this will affect your profits as well. For example, if you see that the company increased their dividend plans by quite a bit over the last year, this is usually an overly optimistic position, and it is best to go with another company to protect your investment.

Income investing is a long-term solution. This is not a method that you will join and then sell out quickly when the market turns on you. The whole point is to provide you with an income each quarter that you are able to use just like any other income that you bring in. The trick here is that you need to be able to find the companies who will be able to provide you with this kind of income.

Dogs of the Dow

Some beginner investors like to work with the strategy that is known as Dogs of the Dow. This is a simple approach that is meant to help you make your money over the long-term. If you are looking to chase the market around and hope to make money quickly, this is not going to be the right option for you. For this strategy, you will look at the 30 companies that have been listed in the DIJA or the Dow Jones Industrial Average. From here, you will pick out ten investments that are performing really well. After you have finished with that first year, you will take a look at the list again, and pick the ten that are doing well for the second year. This does require some readjusting to your portfolio but helps you to pick out companies that are always doing well.

Every few years or so, you may need to make some adjustments and get rid of some of the stocks that you own. You will replace them with new stocks that are now in the top of the DIJA to help you do well. This is hard to keep up with sometimes, but going off that list will make things so much easier.

With this strategy, just like when you pick out any of the other strategies that are on this list, Dogs of the Dow is not necessarily foolproof, and there are times when it is not going to provide you with the return on investment that you would like. Generally, though, it is a good way to find companies that are doing well and can provide you with a good return on investment. If you are a beginner and don't know how to work in the market, or you are worried about finding time to research the right companies to invest in, then this is the right option for you.

The reason that a lot of beginners choose to go with Dogs of the Dow is that it is really simple to understand. You will be able to save a lot of time by not having to look through all those charts, and yet you will still be able to see some good results with your investment. All that you need to do is set aside some time when a new year starts and look at this list. Then you go through and make the changes that are necessary to your portfolio so that everything matches up the right way. There are a few times that you will need to make changes to the stocks you are holding, but many of them will stay the same from year to year, so the work on this strategy is minimal.

There are many strategies that you are able to choose from when it comes to working in the stock market, and we have only brought up a few of the ones that you may be interested in. All of them can be successful as long as you follow them correctly. Pick out the one that is the most comfortable for you and you will start to make a good return on investment in no time.

Chapter 6: Different Styles That Expert Traders Use for Stock Trading

It is also possible to get into the stock market and do what is known as stock trading. Stock trading is a little bit different because you are not focusing on the long-term with this option. Instead, you are focusing on how to make a profit more quickly in the stock market. You will try to purchase stocks when they are low, such as when the company is undervalued or right before the value of the company is expected to go up, and then you will sell them in the future for a profit. This can work well if you know how to read the market and you are willing to take the risk. Sometimes you will only hold onto your position for a day or less and other times you may hold this position for a few months, but it is never meant to be a long-term investment type, and you likely will not hold onto the stocks long enough to earn any dividends.

If you want to go with the option of stock trading, then it is imperative that you learn how to read the market and that you are willing to move fast. You may be able to purchase a stock at a discount or a very low price, and then you must sell it when that stock price goes up. The hardest part is to figure out when a stock is low because it is discounted or the market is low, or when a stock is low because the company is not worth much. If you pick a stock from one of the latter, then the price will never go up, and you will not make a profit.

If you are interested in giving stock trading a try, there are a few options that you can look into to get the most out of your money. As you learn how to use these strategies and get into the market for some time, you will be able to bring your own personal style into the mix as well. Let's take a look at some of these styles and see how they can help you become successful with stock trading.

Position trading

Some of the styles that you can do with stock trading will require you to get in and out of the market within a few days if not sooner. This can be a bit intense for a lot of beginners to the stock market, and you may not want to try that until you get more comfortable. Position trading is a good option if you would like to have some room when it comes to the trading period between purchasing and selling your stock. Many of these trades can last for a few months, and some for even longer.

The benefit of working with position trading is that you will be able to hold onto the stock for a little bit longer so you can watch the trends in the market before selling. If things go south, you will have more time to hold onto the stock and wait it out until the market goes up. There are a lot of sudden changes that can occur with a stock from day to day, even with a steadier stock, and this method will give you some room to breathe.

Of course, this one is more similar to stock market investing than some of the others because you are holding onto the stock for a longer period of time. However, you can choose to make it more of a short-term trade. Instead of holding onto the stocks for years, you may only hold onto the stock for a few weeks. As a position trader, it will become your job to look at weekly as well as monthly charts to help you make some good trading decisions. You will not really need to spend your time looking at short-term price changes with this strategy.

Day trading

Some traders want to work on a short-term investment inside the stock market. Day trading can be the answer to that because it is a fast-paced option that can be hard to keep up with. If you are not willing to constantly watch the market or you are not willing to take some risks, then day trading is not the option for you. As a day trader, it will be your job to purchase a stock sometime during the day, usually in the morning, and then you will need to sell that stock before the market closes on that same day. You are not allowed to keep your stocks longer than this so you will need to sell, regardless of whether you end up with a winning or losing position.

Day traders look at the market differently than the position trader will. They do not care how the stock will do over the long-term because they do not plan to hold that stock for more than a few hours. However, they are really interested in how the stock has been doing over the past few days. When they are able to see a good trend, they will be better able to make some predictions about what will happen with their stocks. This helps them to make some good purchasing decisions.

Day trading is not going to yield you a lot of money off each trade. No stock sees huge increases in prices in just a few hours. But if you do a lot of little trades throughout the week, you will be able to make a good deal of profits from this trading method.

Swing trading

Swing trading is another option that you can choose to go with when you want to get into stock trading. With this trading style, you will purchase the stocks that you want to use, hold onto them for up to two weeks, and then sell them at a higher price. This is similar to day trading, but you will get up to a few weeks rather than just a few hours.

A swing trader will look at a stock and try to determine if that stock value will go up in the next few weeks. Perhaps they have been doing some research, and they see that a big announcement is about to come out concerning a company. That company's stocks may be pretty low at that moment, but because of a new expansion or a new product launch, the price of the stock may be expected to go up. The swing trader would purchase the stock when the price is low, hold onto it for a few weeks, and then sell to make a profit.

The fundamentals of a company are not going to matter as much with swing trading because you are not going to hold your position for all that long. The swing trader is just looking for companies that are likely to see an increase in the price and value of their stocks sometime in the near future. It doesn't really matter to them who runs the company or how much they pay out in dividends because the swing trader is not planning on being in the market that long.

Scalp trading

Some traders will choose to work in what is known as scalp trading. This can be considered similar to day trading, but you will be much busier with this option. Your goal as a scalp trader is to be constantly purchasing and selling your stocks non-stop throughout the day. The main agenda for the scalp trader is to focus on the day to day changes of the stock market because this will help them determine when to make a purchase and when to sell.

The scalper has the goal of purchasing a stock at a low price, and then they will sell it as soon as the price goes up. Since the market is constantly going up and down, this is possible as long as you are able to pay close attention to what is going on in the market. You often will only make a small amount on each sale, but if you do hundreds of these during the same day, it can quickly add up.

Picking your trading style

Above, you learned about some of the best trading styles that you can use if you would like to work with stock trading. Now that you have learned about them a little bit, it is time to pick out the one that you would like to use. But how are you going to make this kind of decision if you have never traded in the stock market? Some of the questions that you should ask yourself when picking out a new trading style include:

- How big is my account?
- How much risk am I willing to take to

make a profit?
- What is my trading personality?
- Do I have any experience with trading or am I just getting started and need to work on something easier?
- How much time will I be able to devote to my trades? Position trading just needs to be checked on occasion while scalping and day trading will require you to spend a lot of time watching the market.

For most investors, the amount of risk that they are willing to take and the amount of time that they have available for trading will determine which trading style they choose to go with. It is not possible for everyone to give up all their time, at least in the beginning, to the trading method, but that is what options like scalping will require. Others may not be willing to take on that much risk just to get a little bit of profit. It is all going to depend on what you would like to get out of this investment and your own trading personality.

In the beginning, just pick out one style that you are willing to work with. In time, as you earn more money and get more experience with the stock market, you can start diversifying your portfolio a bit more and can add in more of these styles to the mix. This will help you to make a lot more money in the long-term, but it is best to start out slow as a beginner.

Chapter 7: Rules That Help to Reduce Your Risks When Investing in the Stock Market

As a beginner in the stock market, it is important that you learn some of the best ways to reduce your risk. The stock market can be a good way to make money, but many beginners will fall prey to some of the mistakes that make this a really big risk. There is enough risk in the investment on its own, so you need to find ways to reduce your risks to make as much money as possible. Some of the steps that you can take to ensure that you are getting the most out of your investment include:

Do not follow the crowd

When you decide to get into stock market investing, you must learn how to make decisions on your own. It is tempting to always listen to your broker or to listen to the friend who has been on the market for a long time. While it is just fine for you to take the advice of others when you are getting started, you must remember that this is your investment. No one else has money on the line when you pick a certain stock or go with a certain strategy - only you do.

What this means is that you can still ask for advice and suggestions from other people. Talking to your broker and some friends who may know the market a little bit better is fine. However, take everything with a grain of salt. You will run into troubles if you hear what someone else says and then jump right in without even thinking about the investment. Always do your own research and use your own judgment to figure out which investments are the best for you.

Pick out a strategy and always stick with it

As you should know by now, there are a lot of different strategies that you can work with when it is time to invest in the stock market. All of these strategies have the potential of making you money, but you need to make sure that you fully understand the strategy that you are working with. If you are not using the method in the proper way, you will not be able to make money.

You also need to make sure that when you pick a strategy, you are sticking with that strategy the whole time. It is easy for a beginner to see a new approach that they think is good, but then try to switch right in the middle of a trade because it is not going the way that they want. This is dangerous. You are never going to succeed when you are splitting up two strategies. There are times, no matter which strategy that you pick, where you are not going to make money, and that is okay. You should just leave the market and call it good, rather than losing more money because you tried to switch your game plan.

You may be tempted to switch out your strategy because you do not fully understand how to manage it or because you start losing money.

However, the second that you try to switch during a trade, the harder it will be to make money and keep your investment safe. You can always switch out strategies when the trade is done if you do not like using the one you picked, but stick it out until the trade is done.

Forget about the timing

Timing the market is never a good idea. There are a lot of beginners who will try to figure out how to time the stock market, but they often end up losing a lot of money rather than earning anything. Experts in all industries agree that it is pretty much impossible to find the exact tops and exact bottoms of a stock, and if you happen to reach them, it was because you are lucky, not because of good planning.

The issue here is that you can't predict how other people will react to a market. You can make some good guesses, but it is impossible to tell for certain when people will start selling or buying a particular stock. If you are trying to buy at the exact lowest point and then sell at the exact highest point, you will miss out on a lot of great opportunities. What you need to focus on instead is finding when the stock is at a good discount for your purchase and then selling the stock when it gets above its market value. This may not give you maximum profit, but you will earn a profit, and it helps you to avoid staying in the market too long.

Some financial advisors insist that timing the market is the only way that you can make a good profit in the stock market. The issue with this is that this strategy is often going to backfire on you. Additionaly, while it affects you quite a bit, it will have no effect on the advisor. If you spend too much of your time trying to outsmart the market, you will be the one who loses.

Only invest what you can afford

When you see a good investment opportunity, it is tempting to jump in and use all the money that you have. You may go out and use all your savings and some of the money from your paychecks this month in the hopes that it will turn out well and you will become rich. But what happens if the investment doesn't go the way that you plan? Now you have nothing, and you may not even be able to pay your bills the next month.

One of the best practices that you can do when you get started with stock investing is that you only invest the money that you would be comfortable with losing. No one wants to lose money on an investment, but it is something that can happen. If you go into the market assuming that you will never lose, you are setting yourself up for a lot of trouble. Perhaps you should consider setting up a savings account ahead of time and putting some money in to help you with your investments without worrying that you are investing too much. No matter which method you choose to go with, make sure that you only add in the amount of money to the investment that wouldn't be disastrous if you end up losing.

Keep your expectations realistic

There are a lot of beginners who will join the stock market and hope that they are able to make a lot of money. They may hear that it is possible to lose money in this market, but they figure that they can outsmart the market and that they will not end up losing all that much in the process. However, this is a bad way to enter the market. Even seasoned stock market investors who have been doing this for years will still lose money. There are many times when the market does something that you do not expect, and you can lose money no matter how much you plan.

In addition, going into the market and thinking you will earn money overnight is a bad idea. Some investments could potentially make you rich, but these are really risky. It is unlikely that you will actually succeed because the risk is so high, and you will most likely lose more money than you can afford to lose.

Going into the stock market is risky enough. Do not make it worse by going into the market with expectations that are not all that realistic. Understand that you can make some money in this investment, but it will often take some time to see that success. You must also understand that there are some times, no matter how hard you plan ahead, when you will end up losing money in the process.

Keep the emotions out of the game

You also need to make sure that you are able to keep emotions out of the game. As soon as those emotions come into play, you will start losing money. These emotions will often lead you to make poor decisions, and you are more likely to lose out on your investment.

This is why having a good strategy in place will make all the difference when it comes to making money with the stock market. This strategy will set up all the rules that you need to follow. It will tell you when to enter the market when you should leave the market, and all the steps in between. It basically outlines what you need to do, taking most of the decisions out of the game and allowing you to keep your emotions away as well.

One thing that you must learn to avoid at all costs is revenge trading. This starts when you end up losing some money on one trade because you made bad decisions or the market did not react the way that you wanted. Instead of just taking the loss and learning from it, you decide that you need to start making that money back right away. You go into risky investment options in the hopes of earning that money back quickly. Often investors who choose to go with revenge trading will not think through their decisions. The only thinking that they do is that they want to earn the money back. They will pick bad investments and not listen to the advice of others along the way. Because of this, they often lose a ton more money than they would have if they just learned from the mistake and moved on.

If you are someone who is really emotional or can let their decisions be affected by what is going on around them, or if you are worried about losing money in the process of trading, then investing in the stock market may not be the right choice. There are times when the market will not behave the way that you want, and there isn't much you can do about it. For these kinds of people, there are a lot of other investments, including ones that are less risky, that can help you earn good money as well.

Set your stop points

Another thing that you can consider doing is to set up some stop points. These are basically the points when you will exit the market, both when you are making profits and when you are losing. These can help to minimize your risks because you will make the decisions about these stop points before you enter the market and money is at stake. If you forget to do these, it can sometimes be hard to get out of the market at the right time, no matter how much logic you use.

The first stop point that you need to set is the one where you will exit the market when you are losing money. While you never want to think about losing money, it is much better to do this before you put any money in. This stop point should be at a place where you would still be comfortable with losing that money if things go wrong. Then, as soon as the market reaches that point, you will exit the market, no matter what may happen later on.

Some beginners find that it is tempting to stay in the market, even when they are losing money. They figure that the market will return and that they will be able to recoup their losses if they just stay in. This rarely ever works, and if you keep in the market, you are likely to keep losing money. With this stop point, you can keep your losses to a minimum and re-enter the market later on if you decide to.

You should also consider adding in a stop point to exit when you have made enough profits. Yes, it would be nice to plan for unlimited profits, but this is not going to happen, no matter which industry you choose to invest in. Adding this stop point in will ensure that you get some profit. Without it, you may be tempted to stay in the market too long, and when the market turns, you may end up losing all that profit and more.

It is best to set up these stop points ahead of time for each trade before you invest any money into the market. This will ensure that you are making logical decisions, long before the emotions can come into play, and you will be surprised at what a difference it can make in the amount of profit that you enjoy with this investment.

As a beginner in the stock market, there are a lot of things that you need to consider. You have to understand how the market works, which stocks to pick, when to get into and out of the market, and so much more. However, if you follow the tips and tricks in this guidebook and stick to the rules in this chapter, you will see the amazing results that you want.

Conclusion

Thank you for making it through to the end of this book! Let's hope it was informative and able to provide you with all of the tools you need to achieve your goals - whatever they may be.

The next step is to take a look at which investment strategy you would like to use when it comes to working with stock market investing. There are many different investment opportunities that you can go with, but the stock market provides the most variety, and the most fun, when it comes to putting your money to work for you.

Finally, if you found this book useful in any way, a review on Amazon is always appreciated!

www.ingramcontent.com/pod-product-compliance
Lightning Source LLC
Chambersburg PA
CBHW030449220526
45464CB00006B/2463